THE STEAMING SIXTIES
Stirring episodes from the last decade of Steam on BR
2. Steam in the Suburbs
Changeover on the GN
By Ronald Wilkinson

Copyright Irwell Press,
ISBN-13 978-1-906919-05-4
First published in 2009 by Irwell Press Ltd., 59A, High Street, Clophill, Bedfordshire, MK45 4BE
Printed by Konway Press.

The year 1963 was a momentous one for steam on BR. Finally, the tide of diesels could no longer be ignored and even the biggest and best of passenger steam power was now only too obviously under threat. This series almost by definition chronicles the decline of steam and on 'the GN' (that bit of railway out of Kings Cross to Peterborough, for our purposes) that decline was horribly abrupt. Steam was still neck and neck (or better) with the diesels at Easter but before summer could get under way it was – gone. Large slices of the suburban services had been in the hands of DMUs even as the decade began but 1960 saw a new Brush Type 2 every week (it seemed) and the last L1s and N2s were routed. I would like at this point to thank Brian Bailey for advice and correction in the compilation of these notes; to me these events are the memories of childhood but he had a crucial few years on me and was/is a much more astute observer. He has in places turned my base metal into gold, though if any of it remains in the wrong part of the Periodic Table of Elements the responsibility remains of course mine.

Socially and economically the year 1960 was indistinguishable from the 1950s and was still somehow 'post-war' but by 1963 London was (to some) already 'swinging'. A handful of main line diesels turned into a torrent and between the Beatles first No.1, *From Me To You* in April 1963 and their second, *She Loves You* in the summer, Kings Cross shed had closed and steam on 'the GN' had been pronounced dead. It took BR some frantic months of repeated stakes through the heart before steam finally ceased to rise from its coffin but it was, to most intents and purposes, over. The last scheduled steam working out of Kings Cross took place on Sunday 16 June; Kings Cross 'Top Shed' closed from 17 June 1963 and that was it. This is what some of it looked like…

Right. The prospect north from Oakleigh Park on 9 September 1961. 61159 spent the great part of its life at Immingham and despite the coming of the Britannias is still slogging up to London in time-honoured fashion. The B1 is on a train from Skegness, an up Saturday working; the first coach carries a name board, which suggests it might be a 'Butlins' special. It was hard work with such an engine especially in these latter days as last-minute substitutes for diesels or Britannias but this was not the longest B1 job, the award for that went to the Grimsby-London fish and passenger trains. A 350hp diesel, successor to the J52 0-6-0STs and J6 0-6-0s of yore, shunts the crated car parts wagons in the up yard, of which more later. By this time it was unusual to see rolling stock in use still painted in 'red and carmine' and although Immingham B1s were daily visitors to Kings Cross, they were normally to be seen on the through trains from Grimsby and Cleethorpes, driven by Boston crews who took over at their home station; up Skegness trains usually had Lincoln or New England B1s. 61159 was only stationed at two sheds in its career, first at Gorton as one of a large batch from the Vulcan Foundry in 1947, divided between Gorton and Sheffield sheds. After the electrification over Woodhead in 1954 they were sent to other sheds in the ER, who were delighted to receive such well maintained engines. Immingham held on to 61159 until withdrawal. In the summer of 1961 it was often to be seen on the daily Immingham workings. Photograph A.G. Forsyth, Initial Photographics.

We recall many of the locomotives at this time as clean, glistening even, but just as many, if not most, were filthy long before the end of steam was even in sight. The 9Fs and WDs of course were malodorous to a man, or engine, but B1s and V2s, especially from that vast, unknown hinterland stretching into infinity beyond Potters Bar, could and did run week after week 'black as Newgate's knocker' as the cockneys put it. This is B1 61093, one of Hitchin's finest, coming through Oakleigh Park with a train from Cambridge in 1959. As 1093, it had been the last B1 to be painted in the original LNER lined black when built; starting with 1094, B1s appeared in the glorious lined apple green, mainly with Gill Sans lettering. The engine was still on the same duties it had been sent to new on 20 November 1946, to replace the worn out C1 Atlantics. In other words 61093 was one of Hitchin's earliest as well as finest! In late 1946 a complete batch of new B1s 1089-1099 and 1105-1107 arrived at Hitchin to rescue the commuter services, but by 1959 only 61090, 61091, 61093, 61094 and 61097 remained to greet the diesels. The bridge had been put up by the Great Northern as a 'public footbridge' back in 1876. There was no access to the platforms and it actually spanned, too, the road on the west side of the station, Netherlands Road, descending by a ramp and a set of steps. The driver of an empty London Transport bus got confused one night and collided with it; for some strange reason, the replacement span was designed by the LMR bridge office, and not the ER counterpart. Unexpected reprieves for steam became a constant refrain during the period, across all the workings. At the time of this view, for instance, the Birmingham RC&W Type 2s in the D5300 series were going back to the manufacturer for modification, resulting in N2 0-6-2Ts returning in some numbers on the rush hour services. This was staggering, when you think about it. Photograph A.G. Forsyth, Initial Photographics.

60059 TRACERY with what would be the down Harrogate Sunday Pullman, at New Barnet station on Sunday 28 May 1960, looking from York Road across to the suburban rooftops of East Barnet. The stock was that of the Queen of Scots Pullman which arrived in London on the Saturday night and could be got to Harrogate and back on the Sunday. It had been stunning to hear late the previous year that an A3 – *an A3* – had been withdrawn. This had been 60104 SOLARIO, doomed by ruined frames but there was consolation in the announcement that no further A3s were in the 1960 withdrawal programme and so it turned out; after that of course it was different. On 26 October 1959, a few days after a General, 60089 FELSTEAD was involved in a collision at Ardsley while running in on a goods train. Photographs of the time show considerable damage to the front end, cylinders and motion, serious enough for 60089's future to be in doubt and it could have been the first A3 to be scrapped. However, the Scottish Region demanded either that 60089 be repaired or another engine sent to replace it. This may have lain behind the withdrawal of 60104 when it arrived for repair at Doncaster about six weeks after the accident. 60104's condition was poor so Doncaster decided to make one A3 out of two, and SOLARIO became a set of parts that were used in the rebuilding of 60089, which was returned to Haymarket after a second General in March 1960. SOLARIO's boiler was also recycled (as we didn't say then) and reappeared on A3 60069, also in March 1960. The rising ground marks the higher slopes of the Northern Heights. Photograph A.G. Forsyth, Initial Photographics.

60108 GAY CRUSADER on the down main at Oakleigh Park, 13 July 1960; the evening light suggests that it is the 7.21pm Kings Cross-Peterborough slow, always a Top Shed Pacific turn. Very often, over the years, it was the first sight we had of a newly returned Pacific from a General at Doncaster. In this case 60108 looks as if it is being given a gentle spin after routine maintenance. It was still not at all clear then, as express after express rolled past with a Pacific or V2 at the head, punctuated by coal trains and freights clanking past behind 9Fs or WDs, that steam had so little time. SOLARIO, we were told, was not part of 'any programme actual or intended', but its withdrawal was merely 'in accordance with a policy of avoiding undue expenditure on steam locomotives other than on the BR Standards'. The crash in traffic and the politically (with a small p) drive to extirpate steam was not yet manifest even on some parts of the railway. Photograph A.G. Forsyth, Initial Photographics.

Blasting through on the down main at Oakleigh Park on Sunday 10 July 1960 we have 60112 ST SIMON, one of a few A3s fitted with small deflectors either side of the chimney, as used on HUMORIST before the war, and the six A2/2s. They were just as ineffective, and were replaced by the successful German style 'trough' deflectors pioneered on A3 60049 in October 1960. The suburbs then were very definitely 'dormitory' in character, much more than they are now. The semi-detached outer limits of London were also less crowded then, with very few blocks of flats and if there were any they were modest in size, four at most maybe, in one building. Houses converted to flats were unknown; such things were purpose-built, and called maisonettes. The only public buildings open on a Sunday were churches, chapels, police stations and pubs, the latter closing strictly at 2.30 (3.0pm in more favoured districts) and not opening again till at least 7.30pm. No other shops opened apart from newsagents in the morning and even they were prohibited from selling a wide range of items. If you'd run out there was no bottle of milk to be had for love nor money and your only hope was to run down a milk float. Having a car didn't help; you could drive as far as you like but it wouldn't matter; garages might be open, but for petrol only. The more enterprising might offer a bar of Cadbury's fruit and nut but little more. And if you'd run out of fags (nearly everybody smoked, let's face it) it meant a trek to the nearest machine for ten *Embassy*; two shillings, tuppence change taped to the packet. Photograph A.G. Forsyth, Initial Photographics.

In the steadily-vanishing little white dot on the black and white telly that 1960 seems to us now, there was little to worry about so far as the demise of steam was concerned. It was regarded as 'unlikely' that the Gresley Pacifics would suffer any losses of note 'for some time' as they were 'still very fully employed on top-link duties'. And so they were; this is 60014 SILVER LINK with an up express at Potters Bar on 16 July 1960 . Photograph A.G. Forsyth, Initial Photographics.

A V2, in a state of filth obvious even from this distance, runs south through Hitchin and its characteristic chalk cutting on 20 May 1961. The Type 4 diesels were woefully erratic in their performance during this time and V2s were often to be found coming to the rescue. The little two road Hitchin shed just to the south of the station is still in use though steam locomotives had ceased to be allocated and it served mainly as a store for redundant Kings Cross L1 and N2 tanks. It officially closed a few weeks after this view, though it proved a useful bolthole for New England waifs and strays well into the following year. One of the new EE Type 1s is in fact ensconced in the shed itself (at least it can be seen on the original transparency with the aid of a glass) and a Brush Type 2 has an up local in the station. Photograph A.G. Forsyth, Initial Photographics.

60103 FLYING SCOTSMAN with an express on the up slow, July 1961. One of the wash out plugs has wept making an unsightly blemish on the well turned out exterior of 60103. It demonstrates clearly the poor water quality that afflicted ER engines, and led to many problems with priming and injector failure. The up yard used to serve as a transhipping point for Vauxhall cars from Luton. In early BR days a J52 0-6-0ST, usually 68827, would come down to shunt the yard, and then work a short train to the London Docks. Then a Hornsey J6 would take a larger train down to the docks too, in the late afternoon. While we still make cars and export them (though they might have Japanese names) we no longer do so in crates. Photograph A.G. Forsyth, Initial Photographics.

60017 SILVER FOX on an up express north of Oakleigh Park on the same day in July 1961 as FLYING SCOTSMAN, unusually, on the up slow; engineering work might be the reason. A Craven DMU moves away north for New Barnet on the down slow. Photograph A.G. Forsyth, Initial Photographics.

60032 GANNET impatiently blows its chime whistle as it is brought to a halt at the Oakleigh Park home signal. Its fine condition shows how highly regarded it still was as a top link engine (note the burnished front coupling) although by 24 June 1961 it would be a spare as it had been out of Doncaster since late spring 1960, when it emerged from shopping as the Kings Cross 'nominated' A4 for the 1960 non-stop Elizabethan. It successfully dominated the service throughout that summer along with Haymarket's 60027 MERLIN. GANNET worked 68 of Kings Cross shed's share with MERLIN running 73 Haymarket turns. It had been thought that 1960 might have been the final year of steam on the train, with trade union objections the main obstacle to dieselising it – how would the crews be arranged? GANNET had been raised from the ranks in 1954 and fitted with a corridor tender, retaining it (apart from a few months) until withdrawal. Photograph A.G. Forsyth, Initial Photographics.

GANNET has been brought to a stop long enough for the photographer to run from the public foot bridge to get a vantage point overlooking the south end of Oakleigh Park station, and catch the engine easing the train away. There is a slight leak from the off-side cylinder; possibly an indication of high mileage. As a result of three light repairs at Doncaster, the engine went 23 months between Generals, unusual for A4s even at the end of their lives. Reprofiling work is taking place on the embankment behind the solid semis of Alverstone Avenue; the nature of the soil dictated that they should be shallow like this but even so the clay still moved in certain very wet conditions. Photograph A.G. Forsyth, Initial Photographics.

It wasn't the suburbs then but it is now. In the early 1960s Peterborough, destined to be the 'southern limit' of steam working from June 1963, was a world away and only a handful of stalwarts/eccentrics made the journey up to London every day; when they did, they often turned out to be railway staff. Now of course electrification has placed it at the outer, and not even the outermost, edge of London's suburban reach. Leaving for the south on 7 August 1961 is 60049 GALTEE MORE, the first A3 to carry the 'experimental' smoke deflectors, later termed simply 'trough' deflectors, from October 1960. The signalbox on the line up from Peterborough East (running under the GN about here) can just be glimpsed on the left. Photograph A.G. Forsyth, Initial Photographics.

Kings Cross on 23 August 1961 and 60030 GOLDEN FLEECE, in suitably shimmering state, waits to leave with one of the famous Doncaster 'Half Day Excursions'. These took place during the works holidays, the trip climaxing with a tour round the works. Top Shed customarily served up the 'spare' Elizabethan A4 for the job; hence the lovely condition of 60030. It had been on the non-stop the previous week and was to have another short spell at the end of August, taking over from 60028, before 60022 was used for the very last runs ever of the non-stop in September; see a later photograph. The engine was as good in running the special as it looks; going down the train was comfortably early into Doncaster and on the return journey regained the 10 minutes late start to arrive punctually, including running Grantham to Hitchin start to stop in 70 minutes 'The Cross' was quite a place in these times with that echoing boom-boom-boom ('puff' couldn't come near; 'bark' was too sharp – it was a majestic, rolling sound somewhere between the two, amplified and hurled back by the vast echo chamber of the roof) as a locomotive backed out with the stock it had brought in. Photograph A.G. Forsyth, Initial Photographics.

Oakleigh Park on 21 August 1961 and 60009 UNION OF SOUTH AFRICA comes through with the up Elizabethan. Haymarket's 60009 ended up the season that year with Top Shed's 60022 MALLARD. The Scottish working of this train could always be identified by the ScR blue background to the headboard, which is very plain in this photograph. 60009 had only just returned from a General on 19 July and this may have been one of her first workings in 1961; along with 60022 it made the very last journeys with the non-stop, on September 8th. The authorities would have liked to have turned over the 'non-stop' to diesels in 1961 but delivery of the Deltics was running late and their reliability was in any case unproven, so the A4s enjoyed a reprieve for a year. Photograph A.G. Forsyth, Initial Photographics.

The North London outer suburbs are a distant memory by now, but York V2 60941 on a down train at Grantham on 7 August 1961 is a reminder of how that shed's 'Green Arrows' for so much of the BR period, unlike any other allocation of V2s, could be found in every corner of the former LNER. They were very familiar in London, where though the engines worked through the crews did not. They were also famously reliable standby engines and it was not unknown for, say, the up Tees Tyne Pullman to arrive at Kings Cross behind a hard-worked York V2. There could well be a couple on Top Shed every day, working in on goods from Dringhouses. Photograph A.G. Forsyth, Initial Photographics.

60103 FLYING SCOTSMAN with an express on the down main at Oakleigh Park, July 1961. At the end of the summer timetable this year the first real inroads were made in the ranks of the A3s, with several taken out of service. This was done to balance the arrival of the Deltics, rather than the various Type 4 diesels that were already around in considerable numbers. The A3s withdrawn were those suffering considerable frame damage from working over the Waverley route as in the case of 60035 and 60079, and also because there was a policy of not repairing A3s from Carlisle Canal. Eastern Region A3s 60055, 60064 and 60102 had excessive frame wear from carrying the heavier A4 boilers. Photograph A.G. Forsyth, Initial Photographics.

60007 SIR NIGEL GRESLEY comes through Oakleigh Park on the down slow with an express, in July 1961. The down goods ran from Oakleigh Park to New Barnet and on to Greenwood until May 1959, and only to Barnet from then. It looks in very good condition for a little-used loop which didn't seem to see all that much apart from the odd light engine. Photograph A.G. Forsyth, Initial Photographics.

60015 QUICKSILVER with a down express approaching New Barnet past No.1 box at the south end of the station, in May 1962. It is hard to say what the working might be, so frequently were A4s and other Pacifics taking over from ailing diesels, though of course there were steam failures too. There was not so much disruption to timekeeping as you might expect, though there were days when everything was falling down around the ears, so to speak. Everyone knew what to expect after a while and 'the steamers' proved remarkably resilient on some Type 4 diagrams. It was when a B1 or a Brush Type 2 took over from a Deltic or a Pacific that real trouble could ensue. Photograph A.G. Forsyth, Initial Photographics.

The startling development at the end of 1960 was the transfer from Norwich to Immingham of Britannia Pacific 70039 SIR CHRISTOPHER WREN, with several more expected, to take over the work of the B1s on fast fish and passenger trains to London. This is 70041 SIR JOHN MOORE which had also arrived at Immingham at the end of 1960, on an up express at Greenwood in July 1962. The tunnel is Hadley South with the new bores of 1959 on the left. Photograph A.G. Forsyth, Initial Photographics.

New Southgate and that long view north, all the way to the Oakleigh Road bridge through which DUKE OF ROTHESAY famously made its fatal side in 1948. A long time after, in May 1962, 60110 ROBERT THE DEVIL comes through the station on the up fast. It's just possible to make out the trolley bus poles on the Friern Barnet Road bridge above; out of sight on the left was the brooding Colney Hatch lunatic asylum and in the distance on the right the notoriously 'rough' district of The Avenue. There, also, can just be glimpsed the 'Top Yard', wherein most of the local coal traffic was deposited. This would be dropped off the slowest up freights, with more coal coming down from Ferme Park with the pilot. There was more coal for the New Southgate gasworks (south of the station, way behind us and bordering on the North Circular Road) which was worked to the Station Yard and transferred. If there was a little bit more at the right of the picture we'd see the familiar turrets of The Railway Hotel. Photograph A.G. Forsyth, Initial Photographics.

An unlikely job for 60007 SIR NIGEL GRESLEY you'd think; a six coach up local – maybe the 'parley' – at Potters Bar on 9 June 1962, though there were many instances of 'fill-in' turns out of Kings Cross during the day. The diesel disruption of the time also shook the kaleidoscope more; new Deltic diagrams introduced in March for a while curiously saw *more* steam on diesel diagrams than ever! Photograph A.G. Forsyth, Initial Photographics.

New England B1 61331 comes south past Red Hall signal box, Hatfield, with train 1B07 on 9 September 1961. It had been at Kings Cross for a number of years but by now had returned to its first shed, New England. Photograph A.G. Forsyth, Initial Photographics.

The year 1961 was to be the last of steam on the 'non-stop'. Three Haymarket A4s were used that summer, 60009, 60024 and 60031 and five from Kings Cross, 60014, 60028, 60030, 60033 and 60022. The last down Elizabethan ran behind 60022 MALLARD on Friday 8 September 1961; this is the engine coming south the next day, Saturday 9 September; this working (and the Sunday one) was not non-stop but the headboard was brought back reversed, like this. Photograph A.G. Forsyth, Initial Photographics.

60045 LEMBERG comes south on the up fast at Oakleigh Park in 1962. It is probably working the 8am Newcastle-Kings Cross, a Gateshead lodging turn frequently worked by one of their low mileage A3s. Driver Andy Robson (*Working the East Coast Main Line, British Railways Illustrated,* various issues over 2008-2009) has many fond memories of driving this train in 1961/62 with the rejuvenated A3s that were great favourites with the crews, as they were comfortable, free running and economical. LEMBERG still shows signs of fresh paint, having just received its last General Repair at Doncaster, with an ex-works date of 1 November 1962. It was one of the last A3s to be overhauled and so survived to be one of the last on the North Eastern Region, withdrawn together on 23 November 1964. The others were 60036 COLOMBO, 60051 BLINK BONNY and 60084 TRIGO. The crated car business seems to be undergoing some sort of hiatus and vans are in the yard instead of the opens. The loading cranes have gone. Photograph A.G. Forsyth, Initial Photographics.

70040 CLIVE OF INDIA approaches Oakleigh Park on the up fast in September 1962, with what would be a Grimsby train. The yard beyond is vacant, to all appearances abandoned, though later photographs of 1964 show it in full swing again. The 'Brits' were universally, almost hysterically, acclaimed by the lineside oiks for (bizarrely, in retrospect) they seemed a bit more exotic than our home-grown fare. It was all very well having these Pacifics and V2s but once you'd seen all the regulars, new appearances were few and far between. In the end, despite being the apple of Immingham's eye, the Britannias fared somewhat poorly on the GN, doubtless due to their run-down state in the first place. Photograph A.G. Forsyth, Initial Photographics.

A3 60106 FLYING FOX looking bright on a down express in September 1962; it was ex-works in June and could have looked worse, for Grantham had few cleaners and its engines suffered accordingly. Potters Bar can be seen in the background. FLYING FOX probably has one of the so-called 'semi-fasts' which called at the lesser stations to Leeds or Hull. 60106 was one of the original LNER A1s built in 1923, and together with 60112 was the last of the ten to be withdrawn in December 1964. As 4475 it was the second Pacific shedded at Kings Cross and together with 4472, 4474 and 4476, took a turn in working the non-stop Flying Scotsman from Top Shed in the period 1928-1936. It is also credited with running the greatest mileage of any of the Gresley Pacifics, 2.65 million miles in 41 years of service. Photograph A.G. Forsyth, Initial Photographics.

A lovely looking Top Shed V2, 60902, seems to drift along the up main at Oakleigh Park in March 1962; the train is recorded as the 273 up. 60902 was one of six V2s fitted with a Kylchap exhaust in 1961; three stationed at Kings Cross, 60862, 60902 and 60903, were the star performers on the Class C freights until replaced by Brush Type 4 diesels in early 1963. Photograph A.G. Forsyth, Initial Photographics.

Oakleigh Park again, and 60033 SEAGULL, in thoroughly respectable condition, comes north in May 1962. Despite being one of most consistent performers in the Kings Cross Top Link throughout the post-war period, good photographs of 60033 SEAGULL at work are rarer than for most of the other nineteen A4s stationed there. It may be a case of familiarity breeding contempt among us behind the camera! Photograph A.G. Forsyth, Initial Photographics.

Greenwood, July 1962. Across and down a slope from the station yard at New Barnet (usually deserted apart from a mechanical horse which never seemed to move) at the far side of Station Road, where the main line ran north overhead, was an unprepossessing gate. To enter here was enter a wholly different world; a path that clung to the line of the railway, climbing up to be level with the tracks under the oaks and hollies of Hadley Wood. You had to lift your bikes over the gate but it took you into the heart of Hadley Wood and the magical approach to Hadley South Tunnel and Greenwood box, with long views up and down the line; trains were close and fast and loud here, separated from the path only by a decrepit wire fence. In the heart of the wood a road (well, a track) crossed high up on Bridge No.45, put up by the GN in 1850 and widened to three spans in 1975. 60014 SILVER LINK is coming south with a parcels out of the Hadley Wood South tunnel; Greenwood box that was and Bridge No.45 lie out of sight to the left; beyond is some of the suburban housing that was allowed to nestle on the southern slope of the ridge upon which sit the well-to-do residences of Hadley Wood. It is painful to observe what a difference a year can make. The previous year, 1961, 60014 SILVER LINK had its last triumphs, shopped in readiness for the Elizabethan and a reserve for the Royal Train. Now in July 1962 she is looking thoroughly down at heel, passing what had been Greenwood with an up parcels. On 22 June 'No.14' had been given a casual repair at Doncaster, but there is little evidence of the care that Top Shed normally bestowed on the A4s. It had recently been in disgrace and a few weeks before had had to be towed into Kings Cross along with its train, by a Baby Deltic of all things. Seeing SILVER LINK like this could have made an acute observer suspect (rightly, as it turned out) that 60014's days were numbered. Photograph A.G. Forsyth, Initial Photographics.

New Southgate in May 1962 with Britannia 70041 SIR JOHN MOORE on an up express, presumably from Grimsby. Immingham, it is said, were fond of their Pacifics but they certainly didn't go out of their way to clean them overmuch, despite a minor outbreak of smokebox door hinge whitening at one point. The famous New Southgate 'ladder' crossover is very evident here; many other stations down the line, like New Barnet, had such a long crossover of single slips, stretching from the down slow to the up reception, laid trailing to avoid facing point locks and detection. It was always a slightly nervous time when the J6 0-6-0 daily pilot had to heave a string of coal empties to the down sidings at about 11.00 for onward transit to New England. See Peter Coster's account (and a good plan of the station and gasworks too) in British Railways Illustrated Vol.11 No.2 of November 2001: *This was usually combined with the loaded coal for Colney Hatch to avoid blocking the mains unnecessarily. The long crossover was a good 300 yards away and, to use it, the main line had to be blocked. It was a heavy pull, and there was no way, other than experience, of knowing that the switches had thrown fully. Judging the margins between expresses and local passenger services was a considerable skill, requiring co-operation with the J6 pilot driver, the shunter and Cemetery box especially.* Photograph A.G. Forsyth, Initial Photographics.

A good-looking 60125 SCOTTISH UNION comes south through the tunnel at Greenwood in July 1962. The new summer timetable had stuttered a bit with the changeover to diesels making everything more awkward; there were diesels piloting dead diesels, diesels piloting stricken steam locos and steam towing dead diesels. Photograph A.G. Forsyth, Initial Photographics.

60034 LORD FARINGDON between the tunnels at Hadley Wood station (the South tunnel is in the background, the North tunnel behind us) on 2 June 1963. By now of course there are four tracks through Hadley Wood and the old single bore bottleneck is no more. It is good to have a photograph of 60034 as it was always regarded as the twin of 60033 in the days when only four of the class were double blast. It was well known by those who had responsibility for locomotive affairs on the East Coast, that they were superior to the rest of the class, and it is no accident that three of them represented the former LNER in the 1948 Locomotive Exchanges. Until the rest of the class were fitted with Kylchap exhausts in 1957, in most years Kings Cross tried to use at least one of their three on the non-stop. 60033 was the star performer but 60034 did its share over the years. In this picture it is running with the tender swapped with 60103; when the latter was bought for preservation, 60034's corridor tender was provided in exchange. Photograph A.G. Forsyth, Initial Photographics.

Oakleigh Park and one of the unlikeliest visitors ever. Amongst the strangest episode of those times, in the last frantic weeks of steam operation into Kings Cross in May-June 1963 was this apparition, Jubilee 4-6-0 45587 BARBADOS, turned out by Holbeck, a died in the wool Midland shed despite being part of the North Eastern Region since the mid-1950s, on 8 June. Its locos went to London, true, but to St Pancras, a 100 yards or more on the other side of the Pancras Road to Kings Cross! The train was a special for a Bradford clothing company and Holbeck, you assume, was simply joining in the extended 'end of term' atmosphere. Stanier Pacific 46245 CITY OF LONDON turned up the next day but that was specially booked for an excursion. Oddly, the precipitous withdrawal of native ER steam after its ostensible banishment south of Peterborough from 16 June 1963 meant that New England was reduced to pinching visiting LMR locomotives even from the North West and Merseyside, to take freights south. This brought hitherto unimaginable Stanier 4-6-0s and 2-8-0s as far as Hitchin as the year wore on. Photograph A.G. Forsyth, Initial Photographics.

Copley Hill's 60141 ABBOTSFORD storming north through the woods in July 1962. Beyond is the said Bridge No.45 carrying a minor road that, in GNR days at least, ran from Hadley (to the right) to Cockfosters (away to the left). By our time it was really a track leading down to the lakes deeper in the woods and seemed to peter out somewhere down there. Far off lie the rooftops of New Barnet. ABBOTSFORD was at Copley Hill from May 1950 until the abolition of steam south of Peterborough June 1963 and was one of the small group of Peppercorn A1s that monopolised the Copley Hill and Ardsley workings for 15 years, beginning with 60118 and 60119 in November 1948. For most of the 1950s the Leeds sheds had four and sometimes five regular workings into London each day and when in good condition these engines would appear at Kings Cross every day, for weeks on end. Photograph A.G. Forsyth, Initial Photographics.

On the same day 60013 DOMINION OF NEW ZEALAND follows on the down fast with another express. Photograph A.G. Forsyth, Initial Photographics.

On the same day that BARBADOS came up to the 'wrong' London terminus steam on the GN could seem as vigorous as ever at Kings Cross; chance could fill the grand old place with steam for periods of the day though that haze in front of the tunnels in this view probably marks the recent passing of a Deltic. In the bright state that Kings Cross maintained to the end, 60061 PRETTY POLLY (an engine we seemed to have grown up with, so ever-present was it) leaves for the north on 8 June 1963. Photograph A.G. Forsyth, Initial Photographics.

Kings Cross near the end, on 8 June 1963; 60130 **KESTREL** was a Copley Hill stalwart and will probably be on her way back to Leeds, though these were unusual times. It was the first built by Darlington and is distinguished by the smooth tender sides, a result of using countersunk rivets. From 1953 60130 was at either Ardsley or Copley Hill, and was never transferred away. The Ardsley and Copley Hill A1s on the London trains were deployed somewhat promiscuously; the A1s at these two sheds effectively formed a common pool, and it was never clear which shed covered any particular working to London, although 60123 and 60130 both had a longer association with Ardsley rather than Copley Hill. Photograph A.G. Forsyth, Initial Photographics.

14 January 1963 saw the bowing out of 60103 FLYING SCOTSMAN in the hardest winter since 1947, when we could have done with every fit steam engine available. But the BRB had made a deal with Alan Pegler to sell him 60103 in working order and everyone was keen to see this contract settled. So with very few days notice the word got round that 60103 would make its last revenue earning run with the 1.15pm to Leeds, with the engine coming off at Doncaster and going immediately into the works to be prepared for preservation. As can be seen, there was plenty of snow, which kept being renewed until well into March. The temperature that day did not rise above freezing but by now the Eastern Region was coping very well, and 60103 was able to go out in style, with its new owner

on the footplate. The engine took 80½ minutes to Peterborough and then 84 minutes to Doncaster, arriving six minutes early to a great welcome. Top speeds were 90 mph at Arlesey, 50 over Stoke and a final 80 mph near Newark. Hitchin-Huntingdon took exactly 21 minutes for 27 miles. Of course the event brought even more enthusiasts than were cramming the platform ends in any event during those days. The Railway Observer: *...the platforms were alive with people. Not schoolboys of tender age, but men of mature years who had travelled from all parts of London to bid farewell to the famous engine, remembering the days of their youth and the eventful past. They realised too, that this was the beginning of the end for their life-long favourites.* Photographs A.G. Forsyth, Initial Photographics.

A busy Oakleigh Park in the last week or so of steam and a filthy 60523 SUN CASTLE running north on the down overtakes a down suburban train (inevitably a Brush Type 2 would be hauling it) on what might well have been its last job, for it was withdrawn during this time. See the earlier pictures of GANNET in June 1961 for the 'healed' embankment in the background. Photograph A.G. Forsyth, Initial Photographics.

A down at heel – down at web perhaps – 60021 WILD SWAN on a teatime train for Doncaster, coming through Oakleigh Park on the fast during the final week. Its condition reveals the run down of Top Shed during the last weeks of steam and shows how quickly the appearance of steam engines could deteriorate with neglect, even if their mechanical condition remained sound, as with the Gateshead Pacifics during the post war period. It had last had a General at the end of 1961 and only spent a few months at New England after Kings Cross closed before going to Doncaster for scrap. Photograph A.G. Forsyth, Initial Photographics.

60034 runs through New Barnet on the up fast in May 1963; Hadley Wood rises beyond. The tide of semis ran north from Oakleigh Park through East and New Barnet to lap against the rising ground of Hadley Wood, where it was firmly held back from the exclusive area around the Common and Monken Hadley. Up there the Battle of Barnet had been fought in 1471 with many of the losing Lancastrian side pursued to their deaths in what is stilled Dead Man's Bottom. The picture is also of interest for the typical 'local gas works' placed handily alongside the railway; they were monumental features and would make a marvellous subject for our card model manufacturers. One aspect we don't miss of course was the stink – at New Southgate it would wake you up if you'd fallen asleep on the passing 221 bus! Photograph A.G. Forsyth, Initial Photographics.

Gateshead's less-than pristine 60023 GOLDEN EAGLE with a down parcels train at Oakleigh Park during the last week of steam. GOLDEN EAGLE had been active (it had undergone a General in January) all the while in the final period, on the York parcels for instance, and though it remained in Newcastle until the end of the summer working that last year, it had moved on to Scotland by October 1963, to be withdrawn from Aberdeen the following year. The last through steam working to Tyneside, *The Railway Observer* reported, was with a Kings Cross A4, 60026 on the down 'Car Carrier Limited' on Saturday 15 June. Photograph A.G. Forsyth, Initial Photographics.

Hadley Wood station in the last week and our beloved 60061 PRETTY POLLY (*rara avis* it weren't) has the 6.26pm Kings Cross-Doncaster, running through on the down fast. As usual it has plenty of miles in it, making the 1 in 200 climb to Potters Bar look effortless, although that would not have been the fireman's view. Photograph A.G. Forsyth, Initial Photographics.

60063 ISINGLASS with an up goods on the fast, coming through Oakleigh Park on 4 May 1963; this is probably 273 up again which was often Pacific hauled in 1963 as the V2s got run down. 60063 was in very good condition having had a General in August 1962 along with 60100 seen earlier. Its seems to have had a particularly robust frame as it was fitted with four different Type 107 boilers off A4s, but survived to be one of the last ER A3s, being withdrawn in June 1964. The 'car yard' is now empty; perhaps the Vauxhall workers were on strike again though the traffic did revive, for a while at least, for photographs in 1964 show it busy again, with the cranes in operation once more. The coal yard on the down side still looks busy enough. New Barnet station can just be seen hazily in the distance. Photograph A.G. Forsyth, Initial Photographics.

A comprehensively filthy 60046 DIAMOND JUBILEE runs by on the up fast south of Oakleigh Park with the 9.40am from Grantham, 15 June 1963. It had been at Grantham and Kings Cross and one or two other sheds for most of its life but had fallen into the clutches of New England in September 1962. It had come back to Grantham a few weeks before this photograph but they obviously didn't deem it worth the labour of cleaning, knowing what was in store for her, and them; Grantham would close within two or three months of steam's banishment from Kings Cross. The A3 was on its last run into Kings Cross, and 60046 was withdrawn from service the next day, 16 June 1963 upon its return to Grantham, in a very different finale from that of 60103. Photograph A.G. Forsyth, Initial Photographics.

That long-lost institution, the light engine, regarded with scant logic as some sort of 'extra' by those in short trousers who sat on wire fences. V2 60814 rushes north through Oakleigh Park in April 1963; it been involved in something of a clearout of Kings Cross V2s to Grantham the previous year and was in Doncaster for scrapping within days – it might even be on its way in this view. Photograph A.G. Forsyth, Initial Photographics.

May 1963 and a filthy, near-black 60032 GANNET runs past the North box at New Barnet on the down fast. Kings Cross was short of power in this period with its ranks of Pacifics and V2s depleted, such that it could rival Stratford at times in the borrowing of engines from other sheds that ventured in range. In this way one of the most bizarre visitors of this period, 70028 ROYAL STAR of Aston, came to work an evening train for Peterborough out of Kings Cross on 31 May. In its way this was even more outlandish (it was ex-WR after all) than BARBADOS on 8 June but was more of an 'accidental' to borrow a word from ornithology, having been pinched by New England and hurled into the fray earlier in the day. Photograph A.G. Forsyth, Initial Photographics.

The winter of 1963 of course had been one of the worst on record, though we probably should have given thanks for the fashion in which it struck down so many diesels and allowed steam to bloom even so close to its extinction on the main line out of London. The new D1500 Type 4s (the Hawker-Siddeleys as they were often called at the time) for instance were virtually invisible. So it really was as cold as this at Kings Cross in January 1963, 60520 OWEN TUDOR making its way carefully out of the station past the then new and now long-demolished diesel servicing shed. At New England since late the previous year, OWEN TUDOR was withdrawn with the end of steam in June 1963. Photograph A.G. Forsyth, Initial Photographics.

60025 FALCON comes north through Oakleigh Park with 1A40, the 3pm Kings Cross-Newcastle train, on 9 June 1963. A Kings Cross A4 for many a year, it went to New England at The End in June 1963 and was withdrawn after a few months. It was a highly consistent performer, always holding its place as a regularly manned engine in the Top Link. It is credited with averaging 60,000 miles each year, the highest of any of the London A4s; it was the only one to come anywhere near the average annual mileages of the Haymarket A4s, the best of which were the 65-66,000 miles per year of 60009, 60011 and 60031. Photograph A.G. Forsyth, Initial Photographics.

MALLARD in the snow, forging north through Oakleigh Park in January 1963. A graphic image of what the 1963 winter was really like over a large part of the country. The Arctic conditions started in the south and west on Boxing Day, and the thaw did not really set in until March. Before she was withdrawn on 25 April, 60022 was much in demand for special trains which continued to run despite the weather. In between she was fully employed by Kings Cross until taken out of service. One of MALLARD's last runs was over Stoke summit at 82 mph with the 2pm Tyne-Tees Pullman. Photograph A.G. Forsyth, Initial Photographics.

60021 WILD SWAN hurries in from the north at Oakleigh Park, June 1963. New Barnet station and the gasworks are clearer than ever in the distance. Judging from the light this is the up White Rose from Leeds which continued to be steam hauled until the end, and was the last named train to be worked by Top Shed until it closed on 16 June 1963. Photograph A.G. Forsyth, Initial Photographics.

Back to the freezer; a V2 moves into the woods north of New Barnet in January 1963. Photograph A.G. Forsyth, Initial Photographics.

With plenty of new work to the track and banking evident south of Hadley Wood South tunnel in May 1963, Doncaster's 60139 SEA EAGLE does its best WD impersonation on the up slow, one that is not so far out in terms of external condition! A number of freights had gone over to diesels the month before but with more Brush Type 4s on coal than passenger work it didn't seem to be going quite to plan. As I recall, the WDs had virtually disappeared by now and the local coal yards would, as likely as not, have their wagons dropped off and empties taken away by a BTH Type 1. Photograph A.G. Forsyth, Initial Photographics.

The East Coast Regions, fortunately, did not (in the main) acquire the habit of pasting, mounting or chalking reporting numbers on smokebox doors. Copley Hill, however, has had to apply a number to its dolled-up 60120 **KITTIWAKE** on a special for the Rugby League Cup Final on 11 May 1963, Wakefield Trinity v Wigan. New 1960s houses, inferior to the 1930s semis are going up, bringing dwellings closer to the railway at Oakleigh Park. Photograph A.G. Forsyth, Initial Photographics.

Our very own PRETTY POLLY, work stained but game to the end, in Kings Cross waiting to depart for Peterborough on 8 June 1963. It seemed endlessly amusing on one occasion when PP turned up at Kings Cross with a pheasant lodged up by the smokebox rim one day at Kings Cross. It should of course have been PEREGRINE... Photograph A.G. Forsyth, Initial Photographics.

It certainly was a glorious day at Kings Cross, that 8 June 1963 – how *could* it last just another week? Unbelievably, even into March there were still steam locomotives to be found on *suburban* work. Not the N2s and L1s of yore of course but sundry B1s and V2s and bizarrely, a New England Ivatt mogul, 43089. Another sighting to leap from the contemporary reports and which must have caused a severe outbreak of eye-bulging was one of New England's clanking WDs heading a failed Finsbury Park Type 2, D5653 and its train. These two well-lit portraits of 60061 that day are a beautiful record of one of lesser lights among the A3s, one that gave over 38 years of service on the East Coast. Photograph A.G. Forsyth, Initial Photographics.

This is the ground immediately south of Oakleigh Park, viewed from the rickety footbridge (known as 'skelly bridge' from its skeletal nature – well, that's how it seemed to us) which formed a pedestrian short-cut between the suburbs either side of the main line. The station itself is behind us as 60054 PRINCE OF WALES, in the sad livery of 'BR Grey', comes north past milepost 8 on the down fast with a short train for Peterborough, on 15 June 1963. This was the last Saturday of steam and the end was very close now. The photographer Andrew Forsyth lived in Gallants Farm Road only yards away to the left, and this bridge was his nearest access to the line, hence the following couple of shots too, also taken on that last Saturday. The A3 might look thoroughly unkempt but, as noted elsewhere, external appearance can mislead, and it had another year of work ahead of it from New England. Photograph A.G. Forsyth, Initial Photographics.

New England's 92178 comes north at Oakleigh Park under 'skelly bridge' on the down slow with one of those famously endless GN freights; amongst the last, surely, on this Saturday 15 June, penultimate day of scheduled steam working. Photograph A.G. Forsyth, Initial Photographics.

In lamentable external condition, poor 60026 MILES BEEVOR is running south of Oakleigh Park on the up fast on that fateful Saturday 15 June 1963 with a parcels from Newcastle (it had gone down earlier in the day with the Day Car Carrier) which it had presumably picked up at Peterborough. It had been at Kings Cross for ever and was thus a constant presence, though it was shocking to see it like this. Photograph A.G. Forsyth, Initial Photographics.

Wonderful view of A1 60120 KITTIWAKE coming through New Barnet in May 1963 from the station footbridge, a favourite vantage point for local enthusiasts over the years. In the days of the LNER streamliners this was one of the places where daily vigil was kept to ensure that there was a complete record made of every working and its engine, until the imminence of war brought the high speed trains to an end on 31 August 1939. These records are in the keeping of The Gresley Society and are available on request. Photograph A.G. Forsyth, Initial Photographics.

Looking as good as ever, Copley Hill's A1 60130 KESTREL comes through Hadley Wood station on the down fast, 15 June 1963. This was almost certainly its last scheduled day in London, though it might well have turned up on one of the many steam incursions which took place over the following months. Photograph A.G. Forsyth, Initial Photographics.

60061 PRETTY POLLY comes south on the up fast at Oakleigh Park on 4 May 1963. Steam on the GN did not simply fade away as it did on some other lines, such as the LNW out of Euston, the locomotives going one by one to leave just the empty stock pilots. It was this that conveyed the vague feeling that it couldn't really happen. So many expresses were steam hauled to the end; steam in fact went out with a protracted bang, a long way from anything resembling a whimper. At Easter 1963, for instance, with the end of steam only a couple of months off, a count of all the principal passenger, parcels and freight trains revealed more than half to have been steam worked, overwhelmingly by Pacifics and V2s. It all felt like slight of hand, somehow... Photograph A.G. Forsyth, Initial Photographics.

And that was it, no more the whoomp, whoomp-whoomp, whoompwhoompwhoomp as an engine, invisible in the ranks of carriages, helped its train out, exhaust shooting up to curl and coil back down the curve of the great roof before the engine shuddered to a halt at the platform end. Well not quite. Steam was eerily absent from the whole of the GN that first day, Monday 17th, but was creeping back by the Tuesday. On the Friday a steam locomotive actually made it into Kings Cross, Doncaster's 60149 AMADIS on an excursion from Hull. It scuttled back north light immediately but the taboo was broken and the *de facto* southern limit of steam working seemed to become Hitchin, and even that was not secure. Breaches were commonplace and the odd A3 was sneaking into Kings Cross in June 1964, fully a year later! Photograph Derek Clayton.